HELEN STEINER RICE

Showers of Blessings

Guideposts®

CARMEL • NEW YORK 10512

Unless otherwise indicated, Scripture quotations are from the King James Version of the Bible.

Scripture quotations identified RSV are from the Revised Standard Version of the Bible, copyrighted 1946, 1952, © 1971 and 1973.

Scripture quotations identified NEB are from The New English Bible. © The Delegates of the Oxford University Press and the Syndics of the Cambridge University Press 1961 and 1970. Reprinted by permission.

The poems in this volume were previously included in the book *Love*.

This Guideposts edition is published by
special arrangement with Fleming H. Revell.

CONTENTS

Showers of Blessings

Each day there are showers of blessings
    sent from the Father above,
For God is a great, lavish giver
    and there is no end to His love—
His grace is more than sufficient,
    His mercy is boundless and deep,
And His infinite blessings are countless
    and all this we're given to keep,
If we but seek God and find Him
    and ask for a bounteous measure
Of this wholly immeasurable offering
    from God's inexhaustible treasure—
For no matter how big man's dreams are,
    God's blessings are infinitely more,
For always God's giving is greater
    than what man is asking for.

Ask, and it shall be given you;
    seek, and ye shall find;
        knock, and it shall be opened unto you.
If ye then, being evil,
    know how to give good gifts unto your children,
        how much more shall your Father which is in heaven
        give good things to them that ask him?
                    Matthew 7:7, 11

Whatever the celebration, whatever the day, whatever the event, whatever the occasion, Helen Steiner Rice possessed the ability to express the appropriate feeling for that particular moment in time.

A happening became happier, a sentiment more sentimental, a memory more memorable because of her deep sensitivity to put into understandable language the emotion being experienced. Her positive attitude, her concern for others, and her love of God are identifiable threads woven into her life, her works... and even her death.

Prior to her passing, she established the HELEN STEINER RICE FOUNDATION, a nonprofit corporation whose purpose is to award grants to worthy charitable programs that aid the elderly, the needy, and the poor. In her lifetime, these were the individuals about whom Mrs. Rice was greatly concerned.

Royalties from the sale of this book will add to the financial capabilities of the HELEN STEINER RICE FOUNDATION, thus making possible additional grants. In the four years of its existence, the foundation has presented seventy-four grants, ranging from three thousand to fifteen thousand dollars each, to various, qualified, worthwhile, and charitable programs. Because of her foresight, her caring, and her deep convictions, Helen Steiner Rice continues to touch a countless number of lives. Thank you for your assistance in helping to keep Helen's dream alive.

Virginia J. Ruehlmann, Administrator
THE HELEN STEINER RICE FOUNDATION

Showers of Blessings

Thank God for Little Things

Thank You, God, for little things
    that often come our way—
The things we take for granted
    but don't mention when we pray—
The unexpected courtesy,
    the thoughtful, kindly deed—
A hand reached out to help us
    in the time of sudden need—
Oh, make us more aware, dear God,
    of little daily graces
That come to us with "sweet surprise"
    from never-dreamed-of places.

Blessed be the Lord,
    who daily loadeth us with benefits. . . .
                    Psalms 68:19

A Prayer for Patience

God, teach me to be patient—
Teach me to go slow—
Teach me how to "wait on You"
When my way I do not know . . .
Teach me sweet forbearance
When things do not go right
So I remain unruffled
When others grow uptight . . .
Teach me how to quiet
My racing, rising heart
So I may hear the answer
You are trying to impart . . .
Teach me to *let go*, dear God,
And pray undisturbed until
My heart is filled with inner peace
And I learn to know *Your* will!

Be still, and know that I am God. . . .
Psalms 46:10

God's Tender Care

When trouble comes,
     as it does to us all
God is so great
     and we are so small—
But there is nothing
     that we need know
If we have faith
     that wherever we go
God will be waiting
     to help us bear
Our pain and sorrow,
     our suffering and care—
For no pain or suffering
     is ever too much
To yield itself
     to God's merciful touch!

*The Lord is gracious, and
full of compassion; slow to anger,
and of great mercy.*
*The Lord is good to all:
and his tender mercies are
over all his works.*

Psalms 145:8, 9

Nothing on Earth Is Forever Yours—
Only the Love of the Lord Endures!

Everything in life is passing
    and whatever we possess
Cannot endure forever
    but ends in nothingness,
For there are no safety boxes
    nor vaults that can contain
The possessions we collected
    and desire to retain . . .
So all that man acquires,
    be it power, fame, or jewels,
Is but limited and earthly,
    only "treasure made for fools" . . .
For only in God's kingdom
    can man find enduring treasure,
Priceless gifts of love and beauty—
    more than mortal man can measure,
And the "riches" he accumulates
    he can keep and part with never,
For only in God's kingdom
    do our treasures last forever . . .
So use the word *forever*
    with sanctity and love,
For nothing is forever
    but the love of God above!

O give thanks unto the Lord;
    for he is good:
        for his mercy endureth for ever.
                Psalms 136:1

15

There's Peace and Calm in the Twenty-Third Psalm

With the Lord as "your Shepherd"
     you have all that you need,
For, if you "Follow in His Footsteps"
     wherever He may lead,
He will guard and guide and keep you
     in His loving, watchful care
And, when traveling in "dark valleys,"
     "your Shepherd" will be there . . .
His goodness is unfailing,
     His kindness knows no end,
For the Lord is a "Good Shepherd"
     on whom you can depend . . .
So, when your heart is troubled,
     you'll find quiet peace and calm
If you'll open up the Bible
     and just read this treasured Psalm.

The Lord is my shepherd; I shall not want. He maketh me to lie down in green pastures: he leadeth me beside the still waters. He restoreth my soul: he leadeth me in the paths of righteousness for his name's sake. Yea, though I walk through the valley of the shadow of death, I will fear no evil: for thou art with me; thy rod and thy staff they comfort me. Thou preparest a table before me in the presence of mine enemies: thou anointest my head with oil; my cup runneth over. Surely goodness and mercy shall follow me all the days of my life: and I will dwell in the house of the Lord for ever.

Psalm 23

The Golden Years of Life

God in His loving and all-wise way
Makes the heart that once was young and gay
Serene and more gentle and less restless, too,
Content to remember the joys it once knew . . .
And all that we sought on "the pathway of pleasure"
Becomes but a memory to cherish and treasure—
The fast pace grows slower and the spirit serene,
And our souls can envision what our eyes have not seen . . .
And so while "life's springtime" is sweet to recall,
The "autumn of life" is the best time of all,
For our wild youthful yearnings all gradually cease
And God fills our days with beauty and peace!

But the path of the just is as the shining light,
that shineth more and more unto the perfect day.
Proverbs 4:18

The Better You Know Him,
the More You Love Him!

The better you know God, the better you feel,
For to learn more about Him and discover He's real
Can wholly, completely and miraculously change,
Reshape and remake and then rearrange
Your mixed-up, miserable and unhappy life
"Adrift on the sea of sin-sickened strife"—
But when you once know this "Man of good will,"
He will calm your life and say "Peace, be still" . . .
So open your "heart's door" and let Christ come in
And He'll give you new life and free you from sin—
And there is no joy that can ever compare
With the joy of knowing you're in God's care.

. . . God is love;
and he that dwelleth in love dwelleth in God,
and God in him.

1 John 4:16

God's Love

God's love is like an island
In life's ocean vast and wide—
A peaceful, quiet shelter
From the restless, rising tide . . .

God's Love is like an anchor
When the angry billows roll—
A mooring in the storms of life,
A stronghold for the soul . . .

God's love is like a fortress
And we seek protection there
When the waves of tribulation
Seem to drown us in despair . . .

God's love is like a harbor
Where our souls can find sweet rest
From the struggle and the tension
Of life's fast and futile quest . . .

God's love is like a beacon
Burning bright with faith and prayer
And through the changing scenes of life
We can find a haven there!

Oh how great is thy goodness,
which thou hast laid up for them that fear thee;
which thou hast wrought for them that trust in thee
before the sons of men!
Be of good courage, and he shall strengthen your heart,
all ye that hope in the Lord.

Psalms 31:19, 24

Blessings Come in Many Guises

When troubles come
    and things go wrong,
And days are cheerless
    and nights are long,
We find it so easy
    to give in to despair
By magnifying
    the burdens we bear—
We add to our worries
    by refusing to try
To look for "the rainbow"
    in an overcast sky—
And the blessing God sent
    in a "darkened disguise"
Our troubled hearts
    fail to recognize,
Not knowing God sent it
    not to distress us
But to strengthen our faith
    and redeem us and bless us.

*Humble yourself therefore under the mighty hand of God,
that he may exalt you in due time;
Casting all your care upon him: for he careth for you.*
    1 Peter 5:6, 7

21

God's Stairway

Step by step we climb each day
Closer to God with each prayer we pray
For "the cry of the heart" offered in prayer
Becomes just another "spiritual stair"
In the "heavenly staircase" leading us to
A beautiful place where we live anew . . .
So never give up for it's worth the climb
To live forever in "endless time"
Where the soul of man is safe and free
To live in love through eternity!

. . . but he that doeth the will of God abideth for ever.
1 John 2:17

For One Who Gives So Much to Others

It's not the things that can be bought
      that are life's richest treasure,
It's just the little "heart gifts"
      that money cannot measure . . .
A cheerful smile, a friendly word,
      a sympathetic nod
Are priceless little treasures
      from the storehouse of our God . . .
They are the things that can't be bought
      with silver or with gold,
For thoughtfulness and kindness
      and love are never sold . . .
They are the priceless things in life
      for which no one can pay,
And the giver finds rich recompense
      in *giving them away.*
And who on earth gives more away
      and does more good for others
Than understanding, kind and wise
      and selfless, loving *Mothers*
Who ask no more than just the joy
      of helping those they love
To find in life the happiness
      that they are dreaming of.

If You Meet God in the Morning, He'll Go With You Through the Day

"The earth is the Lord's
    and the fulness thereof"—
It speaks of His greatness,
    it sings of His love,
And each day at dawning
    I lift my heart high
And raise up my eyes
    to the infinite sky . . .
I watch the night vanish
    as a new day is born,
And I hear the bird's song
    on the wings of the morn,
I see the dew glisten
    in crystal-like splendor
While God, with a touch
    that is gentle and tender,
Wraps up the night
    and softly tucks it away
And hangs out the sun
    to herald a new day . . .
And so I give thanks
    and my heart kneels to pray—
"God keep me and guide me
    and go with me today."

Every day will I bless thee;
    and I will praise thy name for ever and ever.
Great is the Lord, and greatly to be praised;
    and his greatness is unsearchable.
The Lord is gracious, and full of compassion;
    slow to anger, and of great mercy.
The Lord is good to all:
    and his tender mercies are over all his works.
                Psalms 145:2, 3, 8, 9

In Hours of Discouragement God Is Our Encouragement

Sometimes we feel uncertain
And unsure of everything,
Afraid to make decisions,
Dreading what the day will bring—
We keep wishing it were possible
To dispel all fear and doubt
And to understand more readily
Just what life is all about—
God has given us the answers
Which too often go unheeded,

But if we search His promises
We'll find everything that's needed
To lift our faltering spirits
And renew our courage, too,
For there's absolutely nothing
Too much for God to do—
For the Lord is our salvation
And our strength in every fight,
Our redeemer and protector,
Our eternal guiding light—
He has promised to sustain us,
He's our refuge from all harms,
And underneath this refuge,
Are the everlasting arms—
So cast your burden on Him,
Seek His counsel when distressed,
And go to Him for comfort
When you're lonely and oppressed—
For God is our encouragement
In trouble and in trials,
And in suffering and in sorrow
He will turn our tears to smiles.

He giveth power to the faint;
  and to them that have no might he increaseth strength.
Even the youths shall faint and be weary,
  and the young men shall utterly fall:
    But they that wait upon the Lord shall renew their strength;
      they shall mount up with wings as eagles;
        they shall run, and not be weary;
          and they shall walk, and not faint.

Isaiah 40:29–31

God's Jewels

We watch the rich and famous
Bedecked in precious jewels,
Enjoying earthly pleasures,
Defying moral rules—
And in our mood of discontent
We sink into despair
And long for earthly riches
And feel cheated of our share—
But stop these idle musings,
God has stored up for you
Treasures that are far beyond
Earth's jewels and riches, too—
For never, never discount
What God has promised man
If he will walk in meekness
And accept God's flawless plan—
For if we heed His teachings
As we journey through the years,
We'll find the richest jewels of all
Are *crystallized* from *tears*.

*Because thy lovingkindness is better than life,
    my lips shall praise thee.
Thus will I bless thee while I live:
    I will lift up my hands in thy name.
Because thou has been my help,
    therefore in the shadow of thy wings will I rejoice.*
                    Psalms 63:3, 4, 7

The Joy of Unselfish Giving

Time is not measured
    by the years that you live
But by the deeds that you do
    and the joy that you give—
And each day as it comes
    brings a chance to each one
To love to the fullest,
    leaving nothing undone
That would brighten the life
    or lighten the load
Of some weary traveler
    lost on life's road—
So what does it matter
    how long we may live
If as long as we live
    we unselfishly give.

Give, and it shall be given unto you;
* good measure, pressed down, and shaken together,*
*   and running over. . . .*

                        Luke 6:38

It's a Wonderful World

In spite of the fact
        we complain and lament
And view this old world
        with much discontent,
Deploring conditions
        and grumbling because
There's so much injustice
        and so many flaws,
It's a wonderful world
        and it's people like you
Who make it that way
        by the things that they do—
For a warm, ready smile
        or a kind, thoughtful deed,
Or a hand outstretched
        in an hour of need
Can change our whole outlook
        and make the world bright
Where a minute before
        just nothing seemed right—
It's a wonderful world
        and it always will be
If we keep our eyes open
        and focused to see
The wonderful things
        man is capable of
When he opens his heart
        to God and His love.

The earth is the Lord's, and
the fulness thereof; the world,
and they that dwell therein.
                    Psalms 24:1

Lives Distressed
Cannot Be Blessed

Refuse to be discouraged,
Refuse to be distressed,
For when we are dependent
Our life cannot be blessed—
For doubt and fear and worry
Close the door to *faith* and *prayer*,
For there's no room for blessings
When we're lost in deep despair—
So remember when you're troubled
With uncertainty and doubt
It is best to tell *our Father*
What our fear is all about—
For unless we seek His guidance
When troubled times arise
We are bound to make decisions
That are twisted and unwise—
But when we view our problems
Through the eyes of God above,
Misfortunes turn to blessings
And hatred turns to love.

The Key

"Unless you become as children"
And love Me as they do,
You cannot enter My Kingdom,
For the door is closed to you . . .
For faith is the key to heaven
And only God's children hold
The key that opens the gateway
To that beautiful City of Gold . . .
For only a child yet unblemished
By the doctrines and theories of man
Is content to Trust and Love Jesus
Without understanding His Plan.

No Favor Do I Seek Today

I come not to ask, to plead, or implore You,
I just come to tell You how much I adore You,
For to kneel in Your presence makes me feel blest
For I know that You know all my needs best . . .
And it fills me with joy just to linger with You
As my soul You replenish and my heart You renew,
For prayer is much more than just asking for things—
It's the peace and contentment that quietness brings . . .
So thank You again for Your mercy and love
And for making me heir to Your kingdom above!

Blessed be the Lord,
because he hath heard the voice of my supplications.
The Lord is my strength and my shield;
my heart trusted in him, and I am helped:
therefore my heart greatly rejoiceth;
and with my song will I praise him.

Psalms 28:6, 7

On Life's Busy Thoroughfares We Meet With Angels Unawares

I've never seen God, but I know how I feel
It's people like *you* who make Him "so real"
My God is no stranger, *He's* friendly and gay
And *He* doesn't ask me to weep when I pray
It seems that I pass Him so often each day
In the faces of people I meet on my way
He's the stars in the heaven, a smile on some face
A leaf on a tree or a rose in a vase
He's winter and autumn and summer and spring
In short, *God is every real, wonderful thing*
I wish I might meet Him much more than I do
I would if there were *more people like you.*

Be kindly affectioned one to another with brotherly love; in honour preferring one another; not slothful in business; fervent in spirit; serving the Lord; rejoicing in hope; patient in tribulation; continuing instant in prayer; disturbing to the necessity of saints; given to hospitality. Bless them which persecute you: bless, and curse not. Rejoice with them that do rejoice, and weep with them that weep.

Romans 12:10–15

Blessings in Disguise Are Difficult to Recognize

God sends His "little angels"
       in many forms and guises,
They come as lovely miracles
       that God alone devises—
For He does nothing without purpose,
       everything's a perfect plan
To fulfill in bounteous measure
       all He ever promised man—
For every "little angel"
       with a body bent and broken,
Or a little mind retarded
       or little words unspoken,
Is just God's way of trying
       to reach and touch a hand
Of all who do not know Him
       and cannot understand
That often through an angel
       whose "wings will never fly"
The Lord is pointing out the way
       to His eternal sky
Where there will be no handicaps
       of body, soul or mind,
And where all limitations
       will be dropped and left behind—
So accept these "little angels"
       as gifts from God above
And thank Him for this lesson
       in *faith* and *hope* and *love*.

Let brotherly love continue.
Be not forgetful to entertain strangers:
*   for thereby some have entertained angels unawares.*
Hebrews 13:1, 2

On the Wings of Prayer

Just close your eyes and open your heart
And feel your worries and cares depart,
Just yield yourself to the Father above
And let Him hold you secure in His love—
For life on earth grows more involved
With endless problems that can't be solved—
But God only asks us to do our best,
Then He will "take over" and finish the rest—
So when you are tired, discouraged and blue,
There's always one door that is open to you—
And that is the door to "The House of Prayer"
And you'll find God waiting to meet you there,
And "The House of Prayer" is no farther away
Than the quiet spot where you kneel and pray—
For the heart is a temple when God is there
As we place ourselves in His loving care,
And He hears every prayer and answers each one
When we pray in His name "Thy will be done"—
And the burdens that seemed too heavy to bear
Are lifted away on "the wings of prayer."

The Lord is nigh unto all them that call upon him,
  to all that call upon him in truth.
He will fulfil the desire of them that fear him:
  he also will hear their cry, and will save them.
Psalms 145:18, 19

Teach Us to Live

God of love—Forgive! Forgive!
Teach us how to truly live,
Ask us not our race or creed,
Just take us in our hour of need,
And let us know You love us, too,
And that we are a part of You . . .
And someday may man realize
That all the earth, the seas and skies
Belong to God, who made us all,
The rich, the poor, the great, the small,
And in the Father's Holy sight
No man is yellow, black, or white,
And peace on earth cannot be found
Until we meet on common ground
And every man becomes a brother
Who worships God and loves all others.

Beloved, let us love one another:
for love is of God;
and every one that loveth is both of God,
and knoweth God.

1 John 4:7

39

Not to Seek, Lord,
but to Share

Dear God, much too often
    we seek You in prayer
Because we are wallowing
    in our own self-despair . . .
We make every word
    we lamentingly speak
An imperative plea
    for whatever we seek . . .
We pray for ourselves
    and so seldom for others,
We're concerned with our problems
    and not with our brothers . . .
We seem to forget, Lord,
    that the "sweet hour of prayer"
Is not for self-seeking
    but to place in Your care
All the lost souls
    unloved and unknown
And to keep praying for them
    until they're Your own . . .
For it's never enough
    to seek God in prayer
With no thought for others
    who are lost in despair . . .
So teach us, dear God,
    that the power of prayer
Is made stronger by placing
    the world in Your care!

Love worketh no ill to his neighbour:
therefore love is the fulfilling of the law.
Romans 13:10

41

Keep America in Your Care

We are faced with many problems
    that grow bigger day by day
And, as we seek to solve them
    in our own self-sufficient way,
We keep drifting into chaos
    and our avarice and greed
Blinds us to the answer
    that would help us in our need . .
Oh, God, renew our spirit
    and make us more aware
That our future is dependent
    on sacrifice and prayer,
Forgive us our transgressions
    and revive our faith anew
So we may all draw closer
    to each other and to You . . .

For when a nation is too proud
    to daily kneel and pray
It will crumble into chaos
    and descend into decay,
So stir us with compassion
    and raise our standards higher
And take away our lust for power
    and make our one desire
To be a shining symbol
    of all that's great and good
As You lead us in our struggle
    toward newfound brotherhood!

Blessed is the nation whose God is the Lord; and the people whom he hath chosen for his own inheritance.

Psalms 33:12

"Seek Ye First
the Kingdom of God"

Life is a mixture
of sunshine and rain,
Good things and bad things,
pleasure and pain,
We can't have all sunshine,
but it's certainly true
There is never a cloud
the sun doesn't shine through . . .
So always remember
that whatever betide you
The power of God
is always beside you,
And if friends disappoint you
and plans go astray
And nothing works out
in just the right way,
And you feel you have failed
in achieving your goal,
And that life wrongly placed you
in an unfitting role . . .
Take heart and "stand tall"
and think who you are,
For God is your Father
and no one can bar
Or keep you from reaching
your desired success,
Or withhold the joy
that is yours to possess . . .
For with God on your side
it matters not who
Is working to keep
life's good things from you,

For you need nothing more
        than God's guidance and love
To insure you the things
        that you're most worthy of . . .
So trust in His wisdom
        and follow His ways,
And be not concerned
        with the world's empty praise,
But *seek first His kingdom*
        and you will possess
The world's greatest riches
        which is true happiness.

But seek ye first the kingdom
of God, and his righteousness;
and all these things shall be
added unto you.
                    Matthew 6:33

So Swift the Way!
So Short the Day!

In this fast-moving world
        of turmoil and tension,
With problems and troubles,
        too many to mention,
Our days are so crowded
        and our hours are so few,
There's *so little time*
        and *so much to do* . . .
We are pressured and pushed
        until we are "dizzy,"
There's never a minute
        we're not "crazily busy,"
And sometimes we wonder
        as we rush through the day—
Does God really want us
        to hurry this way?
Why are we impatient
        and continually vexed,
And often bewildered,
        disturbed and perplexed?
Perhaps we're too busy
        with our own selfish seeking
To hear the dear Lord
        when He's tenderly speaking . . .
We are working so tensely
        in our self-centered way,

We've no time for listening
          to what God has to say,
And hard as we work,
          at the end of the day
We know in our hearts
          we did not "pay our way" . . .
But God in His mercy
          looks down on us all,
And though what we've done
          is so pitifully small,
He makes us feel welcome
          to kneel down and pray
For the chance to do better
          as we start a new day,
And life would be better
          if we learned to rely
On our Father in heaven
          without asking *"Why"* . . .
And if we'd remember
          as we rush through the day,
"The Lord is our Shepherd
          and *He'll lead the way"* . . .
So don't rush ahead
          in reckless endeavor,
Remember *"He leadeth"*
          and *"time is forever"*!

. . . let us run with patience
the race that is set before us,
    Looking unto Jesus the author
and finisher of our faith. . . .
                    Hebrews 12:1, 2

A Teenager's Prayer

God, here I am in a "chaotic state"
Seeking some way to do "something great" . . .
I want to be someone who contributes to make
A less violent world for everyone's sake . . .
But who can I go to and who can I trust,
Who'll show me the difference between love and lust?
I'm willing to listen, I'm willing to do
Whatever it takes to make this world "new" . . .
But in the confusion and the noise all around
Where can the answer to my question be found?
Dear God up in heaven, hear a teenager's plea—
Show me somewhere what You want me to be!

This Is All I Ask

Lord, show me the way
I can somehow repay
The blessings You've given to me . . .
Lord, teach me to do
What You most want me to
And to be what You want me to be . . .
I'm unworthy I know
But I do love You so—
I beg You to answer my plea . . .
I've not got much to give
But as long as I live
May I give it completely to Thee!

What Is Life?

Life is a sojourn here on earth
Which begins the day God gives us birth,
We enter this world from the great unknown
And God gives each Spirit a form of its own
And endows this form with a heart and a soul
To spur man on to his ultimate goal—
And through the senses of feeling and seeing,
God makes a man into a human being
So he may experience a mortal life
And through this period of smiles and strife
Prepare himself to return as he came,
For birth and death are in essence the same,
For both are fashioned by God's mighty hand
And, while we cannot understand,
We know we are born to die and arise
For beyond this world in beauty lies
The purpose of living and the ultimate goal
God gives at birth to each seeking soul—
So enjoy your sojourn on earth and be glad
That God gives you a *choice* between good things and bad,
And only be sure that you heed God's voice
Whenever life asks you to make a choice.

*Oh that men would praise the Lord for his goodness, and for
his wonderful works to the children of men!*

*For he satisfieth the longing soul, and filleth the hungry soul
with goodness.*

Psalms 107:8, 9

The Meaning of True Love

It is sharing and caring,
Giving and forgiving,
Loving and being loved,
Walking hand in hand,
Talking heart to heart,
Seeing through each other's eyes,
Laughing together,
Weeping together,
Praying together,
And always trusting
And believing
And thanking God
For each other . . .
For love that is shared
      is a beautiful thing—
It enriches the soul
        And makes the heart sing!

What Does God Know of These Modern Days?

He sent His Son to live on earth
And to walk with sinful men,
And the problems that confront us
Are the same today as then,
For vice and crime and evil
Prevailed in Rome and Greece
And power-driven demagogues
Incited war, not peace—
There was violence and dissension
And injustice in high courts,
And slayings were accepted
As one of the favorite sports—
Depraved, debauched, and dissolute,
Men lusted after pleasure,
They knew no god but power
And gold was their only treasure—
So all the things we face today
Are certainly not new
And the Son of God experienced
Everything we're going through—
So let no one mislead you
With that hackneyed little phrase
That there's a "many-century gap"
Between God and modern days—
For God has seen a lot of worlds
In this same tragic state
And He knows that we are headed for
The same, grim, terrible fate
Unless man is awakened
Before the hour's too late
And at long last realizes
That God's always up-to-date!

It is not that the Lord is slow in fulfilling his promise, as some suppose, but that he is very patient with you, because it is not his will for any to be lost, but for all to come to repentance.

2 Peter 3:9 (NEB)

Death Opens the Door
to Life Evermore

We live a short while on earth below,
Reluctant to die for we do not know
Just what "dark death" is all about
And so we view it with fear and doubt,
Not certain of what is around the bend
We look on death as the final end
To all that made us a mortal being
And yet there lies just beyond our seeing
A beautiful life so full and complete
That we should leave with hurrying feet
To walk with God by sacred streams
Amid beauty and peace beyond our dreams—
For all who believe in the risen Lord
Have been assured of this reward,
And death for them is just "graduation"
To a higher realm of wide elevation—
For life on earth is a transient affair,
Just a few brief years in which to prepare
For a life that is free from pain and tears
Where time is not counted by hours or years—
For death is only the method God chose
To colonize heaven with the souls of those
Who by their apprenticeship on earth
Proved worthy to dwell in the land of new birth—
So death is not sad . . . it's a time for elation,
A joyous transition . . . the soul's emigration
Into a place where the soul's safe and free
To live with God through *eternity!*

For I am persuaded, that neither death, nor life, nor angels, nor principalities, nor powers, nor things present, nor things to come, Nor height, nor depth, nor any other creature, shall be able to separate us from the love of God, which is in Christ Jesus our Lord.

Romans 8:38, 39

Time Is a Gift of God

We stand once more
on the threshold
of a shining and unblemished year,
Untouched yet by *time* and *frustration*,
unclouded by *failure* and *fear* . . .
How will we use the days of this year
and the *time* God has placed in our hands,
Will we waste the minutes
and squander the hours,
leaving "no prints behind in time's sands" . . .
Will we vainly complain
that *life* is *so swift,*
that we haven't the *time to do good,*
Our days are too crowded,
our hours are too short
to do *all the good things* we should . . .
We say we would pray
if we just had the time,
and be kind to all those in need,
But we live in a world
of *"planned progress"*
and our national password is *"speed"* . . .
God, grant us the grace
as another year starts
to use all the hours of our days,
Not for our own selfish interests
and our own willful, often-wrong ways . . .
But teach us
to *take time for praying*
and to find time
for *listening to You*
So each day is spent
well and wisely
doing *what You most want us to do.*

Make the New Year
a Stepping-stone
to Growth

Whatever the new year has in store
Remember there's always a good reason for
Everything that comes into our life,
For even in times of struggle and strife
If we but lift our eyes above
We see "our cross" as a "gift of love" . . .
For things that cause the heart to ache
Until we feel that it must break
Become the strength by which we climb
To higher heights that are sublime . . .
So welcome every stumbling block
And every thorn and jagged rock,
For each one is a *stepping-stone*
To a fuller life than we've ever known,
And in the radiance of God's smiles
We learn to soar above life's trials . . .
So let us accept what the new year brings
Seeing the *hand of God* in *all things*,
And as we grow in strength and grace
The clearer we can see God's face.

Beloved, now are we the sons of God, and it doth not yet appear
what we shall be: but we know that, when he shall appear, we
shall be like him; for we shall see him as he is.

1 John 3:2

A Prayer for the New Year

God grant us this year a wider view
So we see others' faults through the eyes of You—
Teach us to judge not with hasty tongue,
Neither the adult . . . or the young,
Give us patience and grace to endure
And a stronger faith so we feel secure,
And instead of remembering, help us to forget
The irritations that caused us to fret,
Freely forgiving for some offense
And finding each day a rich recompense
In offering a friendly, helping hand
And trying in all ways to understand
That all of us, whoever we are
Are trying to reach "an unreachable star"—
For the great and small . . . the good and bad,
The young and old . . . the sad and glad
Are asking today, "Is life worth living?"
And the answer is only in loving and giving—
For only love can make man kind
And kindness of heart brings peace of mind,
And by giving love we can start this year
To lift the clouds of hate and fear.

And be ye kind one to another,
tenderhearted, forgiving one another,
even as God for Christ's sake hath forgiven you.
Ephesians 4:32

A New Year Meditation

What better time
and what better season,
What greater occasion
or more wonderful reason
To kneel down in prayer and lift
our hands high
To the God of creation who made
earth and sky,
Who sent us His Son
to live here among men
And the message He brought
is as true *now* as *then*—
So at this glad season
when there's joy everywhere
Let us meet our Redeemer
at *the altar of prayer*
Asking Him humbly to bless all our days
And grant us forgiveness for our erring ways—
And though we're unworthy,
dear Father above,
Accept us today and let us dwell
in Thy love
So we may grow stronger,
upheld by Thy grace,
And with Thy assistance
be able to face
All the temptations
that fill every day,
And hold onto our hands
when we stumble and stray—
And thank You, dear God,
for the year that now ends
And for the great blessing
of loved ones and friends.

For we have not an high priest which cannot be touched with the feeling of our infirmities; but was in all points tempted like as we are, yet without sin. Let us therefore come boldly unto the throne of grace, that we may obtain mercy, and find grace to help in time of need.

Hebrews 4:15, 16

A New Year Brings
a New Beginning

As the New Year starts
and the old year ends
There's no better time to make amends
For all the things we sincerely regret
And wish in our hearts
we could somehow forget—
We all make mistakes,
for it's human to err,
But no one need ever give up in despair,
For God gives us all
a brand-new beginning,
A chance to start over
and repent of our sinning—
And when God forgives us we too must forgive
And resolve to do better
each day that we live
By constantly trying
to be like Him more nearly
And to trust in His wisdom
and love Him more dearly—
Assured that we're never out of His care
And we're always welcome to seek Him in prayer.

*Come unto me, all ye that labour
and are heavy laden, and I will give you rest.*
Matthew 11:28

A New Year! A New Day! A New Life!

Not only on *New Year's* but all the year through
God gives us a chance to begin life anew,
For each day at dawning we have but to pray
That all the mistakes that we made yesterday
Will be blotted out and forgiven by grace,
For God in His love will completely efface
All that is past and He'll grant a new start
To all who are truly repentant at heart—
And well may man pause in awesome-like wonder
That our Father in heaven who dwells far asunder
Could still remain willing to freely forgive
The shabby, small lives we so selfishly live
And still would be mindful of sin-ridden man
Who constantly goes on defying God's plan—
But this is the *gift* of God's limitless love
A gift that we all are so unworthy of,
But God gave it to us and all we need do
Is to ask God's forgiveness and begin life anew.

"After the Winter . . .
God Sends the Spring"

Easter is a season
Of hope and joy and cheer,
There's beauty all around us
To see and touch and hear . . .
So, no matter how downhearted
And discouraged we may be,
New hope is born when we behold
Leaves budding on a tree . . .
Or when we see a timid flower
Push through the frozen sod
And open wide in glad surprise
Its petaled eyes to God . . .
For this is just God saying—
"Lift up your eyes to Me,
And the bleakness of your spirit,
Like the budding springtime tree,
Will lose its wintery darkness
And your heavy heart will sing"—
For God never sends the winter
Without the joy of spring.

My times are in thy hand. . . .
Psalms 31:15

Springtime Glory

Flowers buried
beneath the snow
Awakening again to live and grow—
Leaves that fell to the earth to die
Enriching the soil in which they lie—
Lifeless-looking, stark,
stripped trees
Bursting with buds
in the Springtime breeze
Are just a few examples of
The greatness of God's power and love,
And in this blaze of Springtime glory,
Just who could doubt
the Easter Story!

An Easter Prayer for Peace

Our Father, up in heaven,
      hear this Easter prayer:
May the people of all nations
      be united in Thy care,
For earth's peace and man's salvation
      can come only by Thy grace
And not through bombs and missiles
      and our quest for outer space . . .
For until all men recognize
      that "the battle is the Lord's"
And peace on earth cannot be won
      with strategy and swords,
We will go on vainly fighting,
      as we have in ages past,
Finding only empty victories
      and a peace that cannot last . . .
But we've grown so rich and mighty
      and so arrogantly strong,
We no longer ask in humbleness—
      "God, show us where we're wrong" . . .
We have come to trust completely
      in the power of man-made things,
Unmindful of God's mighty power
      and that He is "King of kings" . . .
We have turned our eyes from Him
      to go our selfish way,
And money, power, and pleasure
      are the gods we serve today . . .
And the good green earth God gave us
      to peacefully enjoy,
Through greed and fear and hatred
      we are seeking to destroy . . .

Oh, Father, up in heaven,
    stir and wake our sleeping souls,
Renew our faith and lift us up
    and give us higher goals,
And grant us heavenly guidance
    as Easter comes again—
For, more than guided missiles,
    all the world needs guided men.

The Lord is good,
  a strong hold in the day of trouble;
    and he knoweth them that trust in him.
                    Nahum 1:7

An Easter Meditation

In the glorious Easter Story
A troubled world can find
Blessed reassurance
And enduring peace of mind—
For though we grow discouraged
In this world we're living in,
There is comfort just in knowing
That God triumphed over sin,
For our Saviour's Resurrection
Was God's way of telling men
That in Christ we are eternal
And in Him we live again—
And to know life is unending
And God's love is endless, too,
Makes our daily tasks and burdens
So much easier to do,
And our earthly trials and problems
Are but guideposts on the way
To the love and life eternal
That God promised Easter Day.

*. . . [Jesus Christ] hath abolished death, and hath brought life
and immortality to light through the gospel.*

2 Timothy 1:10

An Easter Promise

If we but had the eyes to see
God's face in every cloud,
If we but had the ears to hear
His voice above the crowd
If we could feel His gentle touch
In every Springtime breeze
And find a haven in His arms
'Neath sheltering, leafy trees . . .
If we could just lift up our hearts
Like flowers to the sun
And trust His *Easter Promise*
And pray, *"Thy will be done,"*
We'd find the peace we're seeking,
The kind no man can give,
The peace that comes from knowing
He died so we might live!

*For God so loved the world, that he gave his only begotten Son,
that whosoever believeth in him should not perish, but have
everlasting life.*

John 3:16

Eternal Spring

Easter comes with cheeks a-glowing,
>   flowers bloom and streams are flowing,
And the earth in glad surprise
>   opens wide its Springtime eyes . . .
All nature heeds the call of Spring
>   as God awakens everything,
And all that seemed so dead and still
>   experiences a sudden thrill
As Springtime lays a magic hand
>   across God's vast and fertile land . . .
Oh, how can anyone stand by
>   and watch a sapphire, Springtime sky,
Or see a fragile flower break through
>   what just a day ago or two
Seemed barren ground still hard with frost,
>   but in God's world no life is lost . . .
And flowers sleep beneath the ground
>   but when they hear Spring's waking sound
They push themselves through layers of clay
>   to reach the sunlight of God's day . . .
And man, like flowers, too, must sleep
>   until he is called from the "darkened deep" . . .
To live in that place where angels sing
>   And where there is Eternal Spring!

*For our light affliction, which is but for a moment, worketh for
us a far more exceeding and eternal weight of glory; while we look
not at the things which are seen, but at the things which are not
seen: for the things which are seen are temporal; but the things
which are not seen are eternal.*

2 Corinthians 4:17, 18

The Hope of the World

An *empty tomb* . . .
    a *stone rolled away*
Speak of the Saviour
    who rose Easter Day . . .
But that was centuries
    and centuries ago,
And we ask today,
    Was it really so?
Did He walk on earth
    and live and die
And return to *His Father*
    to dwell on high?
We were not there
    to hear or see,
But our hopes and dreams
    of *eternity*
Are centered around
    the Easter Story
When Christ ascended
    and rose in glory . . .
And life on earth
    has not been the same,
Regardless of what
    the skeptics claim . . .
For, after the Lord
    was crucified,
Even the ones who had
    scoffed and denied
Knew that something
    had taken place
That nothing could ever
    remove or erase . . .

For *hope* was born
     in the soul of man,
And *faith* to believe
     in God's *master plan*
Stirred in the hearts
     to dispel doubt and fear
And that faith has grown
     with each passing year . . .
For the *hope* of *man*
     is *the Easter Story*,
For life is robbed
     of all meaning and glory
Unless man knows
     that he has a "goal"
And a "resting place"
     for his searching soul.

Behold, I shew you a mystery; We shall not all sleep, but we shall all be changed, In a moment, in the twinkling of an eye, at the last trump: for the trumpet shall sound, and the dead shall be raised incorruptible, and we shall be changed. For this corruptible must put on incorruption, and this mortal must put on immortality. So when this corruptible shall have put on incorruption, and this mortal shall have put on immortality, then shall be brought to pass the saying that is written, Death is swallowed up in victory. O death, where is thy sting? O grave, where is thy victory? The sting of death is sin; and the strength of sin is the law. But thanks be to God, which giveth us the victory through our Lord Jesus Christ. Therefore, my beloved brethren, be ye steadfast, unmoveable, always abounding in the work of the Lord, forasmuch as ye know that your labour is not in vain in the Lord.
1 Corinthians 15:51–58

Let Us Pray at This Glorious Easter Season

What better time
        or more beautiful season,
What greater occasion
        or more wonderful reason
To kneel down in prayer
        and thank God above
For eternal life
        the gift of His love—
For in sending His Son
        to be crucified
He granted man life
        because His Son died—
So at this glad season
        when there's joy everywhere
Let us meet our Redeemer
        at the altar of prayer.

Easter Reflections

With our eyes we see
the beauty of Easter
as the earth awakens once more . . .

With our ears we hear
the birds sing sweetly
to tell us Spring again is here . . .

With our hands we pick
the golden daffodils
and the fragrant hyacinths . . .

But only with our hearts
can we feel the miracle of God's love
which redeems all men . . .

And only with our souls
can we make our "pilgrimage to God"
and inherit His Easter Gift of eternal life.

What Is Christmas?

Is it just a day
    at the end of the year?
A gay holiday filled
    with merry good cheer?
A season for presents—
    both taking and giving?
A time to indulge
    in the pleasures of living?
Are we lost in a meaningless,
    much-muddled daze
That covers our minds
    like a grey autumn haze?
Have we closed our eyes
    to God and His love?
And turned our eyes
    from "the bright star above?"
Oh, Father in Heaven,
    renew and restore
The real, true meaning
    of Christmas once more,
So we can feel
    in our hearts again
That "peace on earth,
    good will to men"
Is still a promise
    that man can claim
If "he but seeks it
    in Thy Name."

And there were in the same country shepherds abiding in the field, keeping watch over their flock by night. And, lo, the angel of the Lord came upon them, and the glory of the Lord shone round about them: and they were sore afraid.

And the angel said unto them, Fear not: for, behold, I bring you good tidings of great joy, which shall be to all people. For unto you is born this day in the city of David a Saviour, which is Christ the Lord. And this shall be a sign unto you; Ye shall find the babe wrapped in swaddling clothes, lying in a manger. And suddenly there was with the angel a multitude of the heavenly host praising God, and saying, Glory to God in the highest, and on earth peace, good will toward men.

Luke 2:8–14

Let Us Live Christmas
Every Day

Christmas is more than a day
  at the end of the year,
More than a season
  of joy and good cheer,
Christmas is really
  God's pattern for living
To be followed all year
  by unselfish giving . . .
For the holiday season
  awakens good cheer
And draws us closer
  to those we hold dear,
And we open our hearts
  and find it is good
To live among men
  as we always should . . .
But as soon as the tinsel
  is stripped from the tree
The spirit of Christmas
  fades silently
Into the background
  of daily routine

And is lost in the whirl
	of life's busy scene,
And all unawares
	we miss and forego
The greatest blessing
	that mankind can know . . .
For if we lived Christmas
	each day, as we should,
And made it our aim
	to always do good,
We'd find the lost key
	to meaningful living
That comes not from getting,
	but from unselfish giving . . .
And we'd know the great joy
	of peace upon earth
Which was the real purpose
	of our Saviour's birth,
For in the glad tidings
	of the first Christmas Night,
God showed us the *way*
	and the *truth* and the *light!*

But the fruit of the Spirit is love, joy, peace, longsuffering, gentleness, goodness, faith, meekness, temperance: against such there is no law.

Galatians 5:22, 23

"The Miracle of Christmas"

The wonderment
        in a small child's eyes,
The ageless awe
        in the Christmas skies,
The nameless joy
        that fills the air,
The throngs that kneel
        in praise and prayer . . .
These are the things
        that make us know
That men may come
        and men may go,
But none will
        ever find a way
To banish Christ
        from Christmas Day . . .
For with each child
        there's born again
A *mystery* that baffles men.

"God So Loved the World"

Our Father up in Heaven,
     long, long years ago,
Looked down in His great mercy
     upon the earth below
And saw that folk were lonely
     and lost in deep despair
And so He said, "I'll send My Son
     to walk among them there . . .
So they can hear Him speaking
     and feel His nearness, too,
And see the many miracles
     that faith alone can do . . .
For if man really sees Him
     and can touch His healing hand
I know it will be easier
     to believe and understand" . . .
And so the Holy Christ Child
     came down to live on earth
And that is why we celebrate
     His holy, wondrous birth,
And that is why at Christmas
     the world becomes aware
That heaven may seem far away
     but God is everywhere.

The Priceless
Gift of Christmas

Now Christmas is a season
     for joy and merrymaking,
A time for gifts and presents,
     for giving and for taking . . .
A festive, friendly, happy time
     when everyone is gay—
But have we ever really felt
     the greatness of the day? . . .
For through the centuries the world
     has wandered far away
From the beauty and the meaning
     of the holy Christmas day . . .
For Christmas is a heavenly gift
     that only God can give,
It's ours just for the asking,
     for as long as we shall live,
It can't be bought or bartered,
     it can't be won or sold,
It doesn't cost a penny
     and it's worth far more than gold . . .
It isn't bright and gleaming
     for eager eyes to see,
It can't be wrapped in tinsel
     or placed beneath a tree . . .
It isn't soft and shimmering
     for reaching hands to touch,
Or some expensive luxury
     you've wanted very much . . .
For the priceless gift of Christmas
     is meant just for the heart
And we receive it only
     when we become a part

Of the kingdom and the glory
     which is ours to freely take,
For God sent the Holy Christ Child
     at Christmas for our sake,
So man might come to know Him
     and feel His presence near
And see the many miracles
     performed while He was here . . .
And this priceless gift of Christmas
     is within the reach of all,
The rich, the poor, the young and old,
     the greatest and the small . . .
So take His priceless gift of love,
     reach out and you receive,
And the only payment that God asks
     is just that you *believe*.

"Glory to God in the Highest"

"Glory to God in the highest
And peace on earth to men"—
May the Christmas song the angels sang
Stir in our hearts again
And bring a new awareness
That the fate of every nation
Is sealed securely in the hand
Of the *Maker of Creation* . . .
For man, with all his knowledge,
His inventions and his skill,
Can never go an inch beyond
The holy Father's will . . .
For all of man's achievements

Are so puny and so small,
Just "ant hills" in the kingdom
Of the God who made us all . . .
For, greater than the scope of man
And far beyond all seeing,
In Him who made the universe,
Man lives and has his being . . .
For it took an all-wise Father
To hang the stars in space,
And keep the earth and sky and sea
Securely in their place . . .
And man can never penetrate
The Father's *Master Plan*—
For only God in heaven
Can control the fate of man.

"The Gift of God's Love"

All over the world at this season,
Expectant hands reach to receive
Gifts that are lavishly fashioned,
The finest that man can conceive . . .
For, purchased and given at Christmas
Are luxuries we long to possess,
Given as favors and tokens
To try in some ways to express
That strange, indefinable feeling
Which is part of this glad time of year
When streets are crowded with shoppers
And the air resounds with good cheer . . .
But back of each tinsel-tied package
Exchanged at this gift-giving season,
Unrecognized often by many,
Lies a deeper, more meaningful reason . . .
For, born in a manger at Christmas
As a gift from the Father above,
An infant whose name was called Jesus
Brought mankind the gift of God's love . . .
And the gifts that we give have no purpose
Unless God is a part of the giving,
And unless we make Christmas a pattern
To be followed in everyday living.

Each Christmas
God Renews His Promise

Long, long ago in a land far away,
There came the dawn
     of the first Christmas day,
And each year we see that promise reborn
That God gave the world
     on that first Christmas morn . . .
For the silent stars in the timeless skies
And the wonderment
     in a small child's eyes.
The Christmas songs the carollers sing,
The tidings of joy
     that the Christmas bells ring
Remind us again of that still, silent night
When the heavens shone
     with a wondrous light,
And the angels sang of peace on earth
And told men of
The Christ Child's birth—
For Christmas is more than a beautiful story,
It's the promise of life
     and eternal glory.

A Christmas Prayer

"O God, our help in ages past,
      our hope in years to be"—
Look down upon this present
      And see our need of Thee . . .
For in this age of unrest,
      With danger all around,
We need Thy hand to lead us
      To higher, safer ground . . .
We need Thy help and counsel
      To make us more aware
That our safety and security
      Lie solely in Thy care . . .
And so we pray this Christmas
      To feel Thy presence near
And for Thy all-wise guidance
      Throughout the coming year . . .

First, give us understanding
    Enough to make us kind,
So we may judge all people
    With our heart and not our mind,
Then give us strength and courage
    To be honorable and true
And place our trust implicitly
    In "unseen things" and "You" . . .
And help us when we falter
    And renew our faith each day
And forgive our human errors
    And hear us when we pray,
And keep us gently humble
    In the greatness of Thy love
So some day we are fit to dwell
    With Thee in *peace above*.

"The Blessed
Assurance of Christmas"

In the wondrous Christmas Story
        a troubled world can find
Blessed assurance
        and enduring peace of mind—
For though we grow discouraged
        in the world we're living in,
There is a comfort just in knowing
        that God triumphed over sin

By sending us His Only Son
        to live among us here
So He might know and understand
        man's loneliness and fear—
And for our soul's salvation
        Christ was born and lived and died,
For life became immortal
        when God's Son was crucified,
And the Christ Child's *Resurrection*
        was God's way of telling men
That in Christ we are eternal
        and in Him we live again—
And to know that life is endless
        puts new purpose in our days
And fills our hearts with joyous songs
        of hope and love and praise . . .
For to know that through the Christ Child
        our spirits were redeemed
And that God has stored up treasures
        beyond all that man has dreamed
Is a promise that is priceless
        and it's ours if we but say
That "in so far as in us lies"
        we will follow in His ways—
For God our heavenly Father
        and Christ, His Only Son,
Will forgive us our transgressions
        and the misdeeds we have done
If we but yield our hearts to God
        and ask but one reward—
"The joy of walking daily
        in the *footsteps of the Lord*."

Christmas and the Christ Child

In our Christmas celebrations
Of merriment and mirth
Let's not forget the *miracle*
    Of the
Holy Christ Child's Birth—
For in our gay festivities
It is easy to lose sight
    Of the
Baby in the manger
And that *Holy Silent Night* . . .

And we miss the mighty meaning
And we lose the greater glory
    Of the
Holy Little Christ Child
And the blessed *Christmas Story*
    If we don't
Keep Christ in Christmas
And make *His Love* a part
Of all the joy and happiness
That fill our home
    and heart.

*Jesus Christ the same yesterday,
and to day, and for ever.*
        Hebrews 13:8

"Behold, I Bring You
Good Tidings of Great Joy"

"Glad Tidings" herald
        the Christ Child's birth—
"Joy to the World" and "Peace on Earth"—
"Glory to God"—let all men rejoice
And harken once more
        to the "Angel's Voice" . . .

It matters not who or what you are,
All men can behold "the Christmas Star"—
For the Star that shone is shining still
In the hearts of men
        of peace and good will,
It offers the answer
        to every man's need,
Regardless of color or race or creed . . .

So, joining together in brotherly love,
Let us worship again Our Father above,
And forgetting our own
        little selfish desires
May we seek what "the Star"
        of Christmas inspires.

*In this was manifested the love of God toward us, because that
God sent his only begotten Son into the world, that we might live
through him.*

1 John 4:9

We Ask in Thy Name!

Bless us, heavenly Father,
     Forgive our erring ways,
Grant us strength to serve Thee,
     Put purpose in our days . . .
Give us understanding
     Enough to make us kind
So we may judge all people
     With our heart and not our mind . . .
And teach us to be patient
     In everything we do,
Content to trust Your wisdom
     And to follow after You . . .
And help us when we falter
     And hear us when we pray
And receive us in Thy kingdom
     To dwell with Thee some day.

A NOTE TO THE READER

This book was selected by the same editors who prepare *Guideposts*, a monthly magazine filled with true stories of people's adventures in faith.

If you have found inspiration in this book, we think you'll find monthly help and inspiration in the exciting stories that appear in our magazine.

Guideposts is not sold on the newsstand. It's available by subscription only. And subscribing is easy. All you have to do is write Guideposts Associates, Inc., 39 Seminary Hill Road, Carmel, New York 10512. A year's subscription costs only $7.95 in the United States, $9.95 in Canada and overseas.

When you subscribe, each month you can count on receiving exciting new evidence of God's presence and His abiding love for His people.